NAVIGATING
THE LENDING MAZE

TODD A. SMITH

authorHOUSE®

AuthorHouse™ LLC
1663 Liberty Drive
Bloomington, IN 47403
www.authorhouse.com
Phone: 1-800-839-8640

© 2014 Todd A. Smith. All rights reserved.

No part of this book may be reproduced, stored in a retrieval system, or transmitted by any means without the written permission of the author.

Published by AuthorHouse   04/23/2014

ISBN: 978-1-4969-0023-4 (sc)
ISBN: 978-1-4969-0020-3 (e)

Library of Congress Control Number: 2014906100

Any people depicted in stock imagery provided by Thinkstock are models, and such images are being used for illustrative purposes only.
Certain stock imagery © Thinkstock.

This book is printed on acid-free paper.
Because of the dynamic nature of the Internet, any web addresses or links contained in this book may have changed since publication and may no longer be valid. The views expressed in this work are solely those of the author and do not necessarily reflect the views of the publisher, and the publisher hereby disclaims any responsibility for them.

INTRODUCTION

The time has come to either start a business or expand an existing business. If you are like most individuals you will need funds to do so. One such means to start or expand a business is through borrowing money. Even the largest of companies need to borrow money to begin operations or expand their current operations. The only difference between them and you is their experience in navigating the loan process.

Most if not all of us have seen a child's maze. The one's where there is a beginning and an end with numerous dead-ends in between and the child needs to locate the most effective and efficient route to locate the exit of the maze. At times the child gets frustrated and quits; other times he or she loses valuable time in locating the exit. That visual description is exactly like the lending experience.

The lending process has always been a maze and after the recession of 2008, 2009 and beyond the maze has become increasingly difficult to navigate. The government has added additional regulations for the banks to comply with, subsequently causing the banks to tighten their due diligence process and loan standards. All of which have added turn-offs in the loan maze for the borrower to work through. If the turn-offs do not prevent you from obtaining a loan altogether, they will at the very least delay the process. The most effective way to prevent either one from happening is through careful preparation. Diligent preparation will minimize the chances of either one from happening.

Business owners know their business inside and out until they become experts in their field. Whether one is in the retail business, the restaurant business, the hotel business or any of the other businesses that make-up this economy, very few business owners borrow money on a regular basis. Between each loan the lending process changes as everything has changed, leaving the business owner somewhat naïve and confused over the most recent process.

Coming from an entrepreneurial family I remember my father telling me in the 1950's if his cash flow was too weak to cover payroll, he could walk into the bank, speak to the manager, or maybe the owner at the time. (Back in the 1950's banks were frequently owned by other local business owners.) The manager would walk over to the tellers, have them advance my father the money, telling him to return on Monday to sign the paperwork. A bank manager couldn't do that today if he or she wanted to.

That was the 1950's, which is over 60 years ago. As with everything, business has evolved. Even compared to the economic robust early 2000's the lending environment has drastically changed. The most effective way for a business owner to participate in the lending marketplace and obtain the desired outcome is to thoroughly understand it and thoroughly prepare for it.

Why Are Banks So Risk Averse?

Frequently borrowers ask, "Why are banks so risk averse?" The question is way too broad, as each individual bank has its own lending requirements. What may appear to be a risky loan to one bank is an acceptable loan to another. Another question a business owner needs to ask him or her self: is this project one that is suited for a loan or, should the project be presented to an angel investor or venture capital company?

Banks lend within certain lending parameters. The parameters are established by both the bank's charter and/or the bank's policy makers. Some of the parameters may include the maximum size of any loan, the maximum lending to any one client inclusive of all of its loans, minimum credit score, the minimum debt service coverage ratio and minimum capital requirements. Loans that do not fall within these parameters are declined.

Other than during the economic crisis in the late 2000's, banks very much want to loan money. Lending is the primary profit center for banks. Banks not continually initiating and finalizing loans is much like a clothing store not having customers buying the clothes or, any store with its doors open not selling what it opened their its doors to sell.

My Side, Your Side

Every transaction in business needs to create a win-win outcome for both parties to be satisfied with the purchase. For example, when a buyer walks into a store and purchases clothes and the buyer becomes satisfied with the style, color and price, and the store owner is satisfied with the price established for the clothes, the clothes are ultimately purchased and all parties in the transaction are satisfied. The same is true for an automobile purchase, even though this is more complicated than a purchase of an article of clothing, considering the price, complexity of the automobile purchase, service and other factors. A house purchase becomes even more complicated, as one needs to determine both one's short term and long-term needs along with the price. Needs may require schools for one's children, travel time to work, concerns for traffic, parks or other recreational facilities, taxes, etc.

> " The trick is in what one emphasizes. We either make ourselves miserable, or we make ourselves strong. The amount of work is the same. "
>
> - Carlos Castaneda

Loans are not any different. A loan is a transaction that has two parties and each party needs to make money from the loan transaction. The bank makes money through interest payments and the borrower's intent is to make more money than the total of all of the loan payments. A business owner needs to look at the money he or she borrows as an "investment" and should anticipate having a return on that investment. When a business loan is for business growth, the growth of the business and subsequent profit should be larger than the principal and interest payments. When a loan is to restructure debt, there should be a reduction in loan payments. This difference in the existing loan payments and new

TODD A. SMITH

loan payments is the first return on investment. How one handles the business moving forward with reduced loan payments will be the second return on investment.

The first step in obtaining a win-win outcome is to decide where to apply for a loan. Choosing the correct lending institution to apply for funding will also have an effect on the type of funding a business will obtain. Different lending institutions have expertise in different types of loans, as well as differing lending criteria.

Let's compare obtaining a loan to shopping for clothes. One of the first decisions a person makes when they shop for clothes is the store they want to shop at. The store decision is based upon the event or the location where the clothes will be worn. This may seem simple--or is it? A clothing staple for most women's closets is a black dress. The event where the dress will be worn will determine where one shops for the dress. If the event is meeting your boyfriend's parents for the first time, more specifically at a family gathering that includes his extended family, you very much want to look appropriate. Will you be shopping at Macy's, Victoria's Secret or a Little Black Dress Shop on the internet? Fast forward six months: you are now going on a romantic weekend with your boyfriend. A black dress will be perfect for a night on the town; the same dinner dress, or something a little different? What does this story have to do with a loan? The correct lending institution is as important to one's success and current circumstances. Not all loans and lending institutions are created equal. Just as shopping at the wrong store for the black dress could have poor results, the same holds true when applying for a loan. Applying for a loan at the wrong institution may not result in the desired outcome.

For any transaction to be a very successful transaction, it needs to be a win-win for everyone. A win-win means the client needs to be happy with the process and the outcome, and the lender needs to be satisfied with the client and the profit.

Let's take the car purchase. Everyone would like to purchase his or her dream car right out of the gate. A person's first car: is the car a Corvette, a Cadillac, or maybe a person's first Mercedes-Benz? The car they have waited a whole "life-time for". A life-time at that moment could be anywhere from 16-18 years. One that strikes their fancy. For me, I was one of the lucky ones. I purchased my dream car at car number 2. My first car was a 1969 Ford Galaxy 500--not exactly the car for a "hip" kid from Jersey. Well I hit pay dirt with car number 2, a 1972 MGBGT. For those who do not know what type of car this was, it was a car built in Great Britain by a manufacturer named British Leyland. It was a car for all of us "cool-cats". The moral of this story; your first loan may not be perfect or have the exact terms you are looking for, but it serves the purpose, to move your business to the next step. I am confident the person selling me my first car would have liked to have made a larger and more profitable transaction, but the transaction worked for both of us and it was a win-win. The car, as "old" at is may have appeared, served the purpose.

Why should a business owner utilize the services of a loan intermediary?

Why should a business owner utilize the services of a loan intermediary? The simple answer is expertise, and an experienced loan intermediary has vast amounts of it. His or her expertise will come in the form of how to analyze your company's past, present and, future; the most effective means in which to package the loan and where to place the loan for the best possibility of success. The most effective financing for your company may be from an institution a borrower may have never heard of or, a form of financing a borrower may have never been exposed to.

Companies and individuals hire general contractors to coordinate the construction of their buildings and a good one will make the construction process appear seamless. A qualified automobile mechanic will be able to repair your car in a much shorter time frame than a novice, particularly with today's cars and trucks. That one tool the mechanic has within his possession or the frequency in which an automobile technician has performed a specific repair makes all the difference in the efficiency of how a repair is accomplished.

The lending environment is ever changing and, lenders' criteria are ever evolving as well. An experienced, well-qualified loan intermediary's knowledge of these changes is vital to the success of a borrower's loan and the efficiency with which it is completed.

Many businesses require approval from town zoning boards for the purpose of moving their businesses to a specific location or, to construct a building to certain specifications or something as simple as constructing a new sign to make people passing by notice your company. These boards have the power to approve or deny your business expansion. Almost every business hires an attorney to accomplish the task at hand for their expertise to arrive at the desired outcome.

The attorneys know the board and have a working knowledge of what parameters in which they will approve an application and those in which they will not. An experienced attorney will also know how to present his or her case to the board, to be prepared for the questions his or her experience anticipates board members will ask. He or she must be able to correctly explain the positives of the company and its impact on the community while appropriately addressing any of the negative concerns a board may raise. A good attorney will also have prepared its client on any compromises that may present themselves. An experienced attorney will have a high success rate. There are very few businesses that will take this presentation upon themselves. First, they understand the importance of obtaining the variance for the growth of their company and they understand the manner in which their case is presented will only enhance their chances of obtaining the desired outcome.

> **The man who will use his skill and constructive imagination to see how much he can give for a dollar, instead of how little he can give for a dollar, is bound to succeed.**
>
> *- Henry Ford*

Hiring a loan intermediary very much parallels the above, though there are some nuances that change the details. The first nuance is that the business owner will never directly present his or her loan in front of a loan committee, and more than likely will never know who sits on the loan committee. The second nuance is that a borrower will have an opportunity to obtain a loan from a lending institution outside of its general geographic location, which may have an expertise in a specific genre of business or type of financing. With today's communications many lenders are lending outside of a reasonable geographic area of a bank branch. This increases the opportunities for obtaining financing, as it will provide a larger array of lenders to present the loan opportunity to. A qualified loan intermediary will know who the lenders are, what their lending forte is and how to correctly package or present the loan in a very parallel manner to how an attorney makes his case to one of the local boards.

Carrying over our jury scenario from the previous section, there are many opportunities for people to defend themselves in court and many persons elect to be represented by an attorney, even in cases that may not require an attorney. The reason why? . . . To increase their chances to obtain the outcome they so very much want. The major difference between court and a bank is this: when being represented by an attorney, usually one wants to remain where they are. What does that mean? For example, you are driving down the road listening to the radio, enjoying a recent success in life, never paying attention to speed limit signs. Oops, you are speeding, not just speeding a little bit, but 25 miles over the speed limit. It's a large enough spread between the speed limit and your actual speed where the cost of the ticket, possible loss of license and increased insurance costs could be substantial. Is the person who was speeding required to be represented by an attorney? Probably not. Does he or she elect to be represented by an attorney? More than likely, yes. Because, they want to put themselves in the best possible position to obtain the desired outcome. That outcome would be the reduction of the charge or eliminating it altogether, minimize the damage. In this scenario, it's negating the long-term effect of a speeding ticket. The attorney brings the expertise to accomplish that task. In other words, he or she obtains a result with minimal to no negative impact.

Obtaining a loan is somewhat different. Instead of preventing a negative impact on your life, the loan will provide a positive impact on your business and your future. The loan will advance your objectives. That is the reason business owners utilize the services of a person or company to assist them in their endeavors. The expense at the beginning amortized over the life of the loan is minimal.

Another reason many persons engage the services of a loan intermediary other than experience is time. The loan process can be very time consuming, and by engaging an expert, it allows the business owner to do what he or she does best-- and that is to run his or her own company. Now, let's walk through the steps you need to take and the documents you need to prepare in order to successfully navigate the loan maze.

1. GENERAL INFORMATION FORM

The General Information Form is just as the name describes. It is a form that provides general information on the borrower and the project for which the funds are being requested.

This is the form where you will provide your "name, rank and serial number". Some of the information may seem redundant to information that is included in other documents provided. The information in the other sections will be much more specific and expand on information in the General Information Form.

- CompanyName
- Company Owner's Name

- Address
- Telephone Number

- Project Description
- Loan Amount Request

2. OWNERSHIP AND MANAGEMENT BIOGRAPHIES

This is an intrinsic portion of the loan process which does not have a numeric qualifier. A person's background or biography is provided almost every time a person changes his or her situation in life.

In the music business, when one desires to become a member of an established orchestra or enter a college music program there will be auditions required, just as sports teams have tryouts. When applying for a job one will need to go through the interview process and, scholastic masters or doctorate degree programs have their pre-qualification criteria as well. All of these programs want to know where you are in the knowledge and/or talent process. The loan process is very parallel to all of the above.

NAVIGATING THE LENDING MAZE

Whether you are starting a business, buying an existing business, expanding your business or, just purchasing property to operate your business from, providing the lending institution with your background and biography is a part of the loan application process. When writing one's biography one should keep in mind the question the bank personnel will be asking themselves during underwriting; is there enough talent within the company to make the company continually successful and profitable?

Business owners should not be taken aback when a lender asks for one's biography, background or skill set. A lender wants to know who you are and you should take this opportunity to provide details on yourself and your management's qualifications.

Small business owners require two different types of skill sets: the first is the ability to perform the task which the company provides, such as manufacturing a product, repairing automobiles or providing any type of service. The second skill set is the ability to operate a profitable business. Yes, the two are completely different. The biographies need to highlight one's talents within each category.

Different scenarios require different narratives of one's skill set or biography. For example: a successful business owner applying for a loan to purchase a building in which they will permanently house their business requires a different type of biography than a corporate executive purchasing his or her business for the first time. The existing business owner who has a track record of success will write a narrative describing it. A former corporate executive purchasing his or her first business will need to describe what are considered cross-over skills. Cross-over skills are business attributes and knowledge that can be easily transferred to the operation of another business or, a different type of business than one has previously been employed in. This type of a biography requires some forethought. The skills will need to be expressed focusing on how they relate to the new business.

The same can be said for the complexities of a business. A custom valve manufacturer which requires a finite knowledge of design, manufacturing and the application of the final product will need to provide details on all of the key persons involved. The reason being, those persons will be difficult to replace and ultimately have an effect on the profitability of the business. Businesses such as surgery centers that require licenses to operate will need to be the most specific on the biographies. The inability to obtain a license or the loss of an operating license will ultimately shut a company down, thus causing an interruption in the cash flow and risk being unable to fulfill the loan obligation. Those companies that employ persons with a less complex skill set can be less specific in the biographies of key employees.

3. PERSONAL TAX RETURNS

Needless to say everyone knows what personal tax returns are.

Lending institutions will require the past three years of tax returns for all of those persons who own 20% or more of the business the loan has been applied for. If the financially strongest partner or an owner with the strongest credit rating owns less than 20% of the company their tax returns could be requested as well.

The banks require three years of tax returns because the income noted on the returns will be the income used as the income of the borrower during the loan process. The second reason the lender requests three years of tax returns is because they are looking for trends in the borrower's financial situation. The trends will be stability, a growth curve or a decrease in income. The lending institutions will also be looking to see if there are large erratic swings in income. When tax returns are requested, the banks want all of the schedules-- not just the first few pages or compilation pages. The information on the tax returns will be verified against all of the other applicable financial data submitted

Along with the tax returns somewhere during the loan process an IRS form 4506-T will need to be signed. Form 4506-T is a form that allows the bank to request a copy of your tax return from the IRS for the purpose of verifying the tax returns submitted by the borrower, if the need arises.

4. PERSONAL FINANCIAL STATEMENTS

A Personal Financial Statement or PFS, as it is often referred to, is to an individual what a balance sheet, income statement and cash flow analysis is to a business. The personal financial statement will provide a snap-shot into one's personal finances.

The first section of a PFS is the personal information and the date when the PFS has been completed. There are two sections for names. Husbands and wives need to submit one PFS. Persons who are applying for a loan together and are not married must submit individual PFS's. The date may not seem important because we date everything in life. With a PFS the date is more important than one would think because, most if not all lending institutions will require the PFS not to be any older than 60 or 90 days. The necessity to have a personal financial statement on record no older than 60 or 90 days at times is an internal bank requirement. With the SBA, it is required by their rules and regulations. This means if the loan process takes longer than 60 or 90 days a personal financial statement may need to be updated or resubmitted.

What may change during a 60-90 day period to require an updated financial statement?

- Mortgages may be paid off
- stock and investment portfolios both rise and fall
- people lose their jobs or obtain a promotion including a raise

A lending institution wants to have one's financial snapshot reflecting current information, as close to finalizing a loan as possible.

The second part of the personal financial statement is the Income Statement or Cash Flow Analysis. This section of the PFS will determine whether or not one has a positive or negative cash flow. A positive cash flow means you have more income than expenses and a negative cash flow means you have the opposite. All income and expenses will need to be documented on this section of the PFS. All income meaning: salary, bonuses, rental income, dividends, partnership income, investment income and any other. These should be listed as your gross income; taxes are dealt with under one's liabilities. The incomes section noted as "Other" can include such items as alimony, child support, trust fund income, etc., some of which will be at the borrower's discretion on whether they wish to disclose them or not.

On the right side of the income statement portion of the PFS is where one lists all liabilities. Include liabilities such as mortgage or rent payments, federal, state and local tax liabilities, all loans such as credit card, auto loans, and student loans, etc.

Both the income and expenses should be noted as yearly expenses. The expenses noted on the right are then deducted against the total income noted on the left and one's current cash flow is noted.

As noted on the top of this section again there is a spot in which to place the date, which indicates the income is as of that specific date.

Directly underneath the income statement is a check off for the question on whether or not you anticipate a change in your situation in the next 12 months. This change can be for several different items such as inheritance, promotion and raise or the finalizing of a business or real estate sale, just to name a few. In the event one checks this box an explanation will need to be submitted along with the PFS.

The next section of the PFS is the balance sheet. This will list all of one's assets and liabilities. The assets will include such items as real estate, both residential and commercial, available cash, investments, securities, retirement plans, life insurance cash, notes payable to you from others, just to name a few. The Liabilities section will list all of one's financial obligations whether they are secured or unsecured. **The difference between assets and liabilities is a person's net worth**.

With the submission of a PFS, the borrower should include the most recent investment statement from any and all investment companies.

5. SALES CONTRACT:

The most significant sales contract will most likely be a sales contract to purchase property or a business. A sales contract for either purchase should be executed prior to the loan application. The sales contract will provide details to the lending institution on the amount of money required to consummate a transaction and the size of down payment or capital infusion of the borrower. Other sales contracts that may be part of the loan process could be for equipment, inventory, and furniture or, contracts from your customers to purchase the borrowing company's product or service.

The sales contract to purchase property or a business will need to have flexibility within the terms as it pertains to obtaining financing for the

NAVIGATING THE LENDING MAZE

purchase. Over the years it has been customary to put into a contract a 30 day clause to obtain financing or an LOI (Letter of Intent) and 15 days to close, for a total of 45 days to finalize the financing. In the current lending environment 45 days is not long enough to obtain a commercial loan. Due to regulatory changes and increased government scrutiny, loans now can at times take upwards of 6 months to finalize.

Not being able to obtain financing within the contract time frame is not a reflection of the finances of the buyer. It is more of a reflection of the lending environment which currently exists.

This specific section usually applies to contracts that pertain to real estate and/or business purchases. Some other contracts that should be submitted when they are part of a business transaction could include a franchise agreement or an executed contract for the goods or services that the borrowing company provides.

6. PICTURES

This section of the application process is somewhat self-explanatory. The lender will require photographs of the interior and exterior of the property being financed when purchasing real estate.

> **"** To succeed... You need to find something to hold on to, something to motivate you, something to inspire you. **"**
>
> - *Tony Dorsett*

If the loan is for the purchase of equipment a picture of the equipment should be included. Manufacturing companies should include a picture of their product as well as photographs of the manufacturing process from raw material to the final product.

7. CONSTRUCTION INFORMATION:

If one's loan application is going to require funds for construction there are several details that will need to be included with the application. If proceeds from the loan will not be used for construction this section can be ignored.

Even minor renovations can increase the value of a building and noting the renovations in the loan process will have a positive effect on the appraisal. An appraisal that is based upon a project that is going to be renovated will include two values. One value will be an "as-is" value. This is the value of the building in its current condition. The second value will be an "as-completed" value. This will be the value of the building when all of the renovations have been completed.

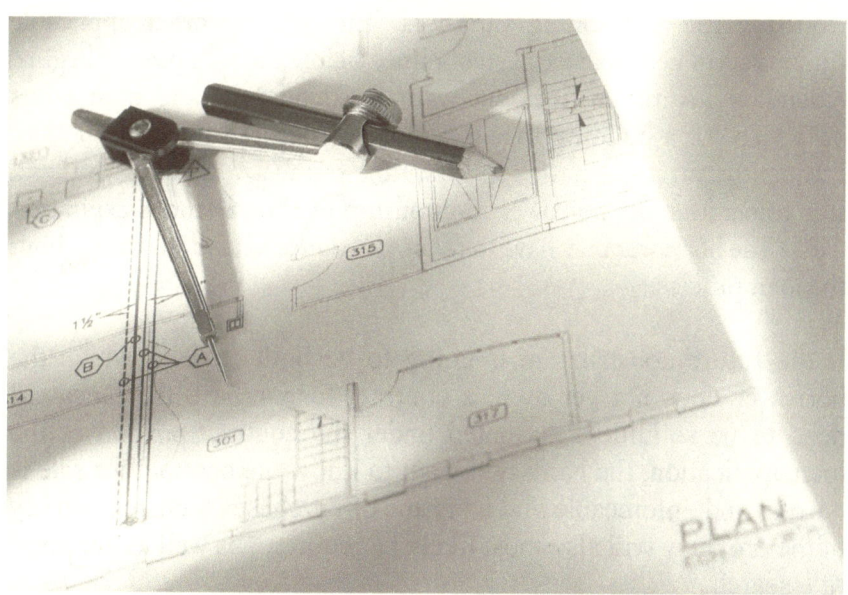

The extent of the construction will determine the amount of construction documentation required. When the construction of a building is going to be minimal the required documentation will include detailed contractor estimates. The contractors will need to be licensed in their applicable trades. Based upon the extent of the minimal construction, architectural drawings by a licensed architect may or may not be required. Each governmental jurisdiction has different building codes and protocol.

Major renovations of an existing building or the construction of a new building, which is frequently called "ground-up" construction, requires much more detailed information. Full sets of architectural drawings will need to be submitted along with a detailed general contractor's cost estimate. When choosing a general contractor for a bank funded construction project it is recommended one chooses a very experienced contractor. The probability the bank will require a surety and completion bond from the contractor is very high. This protects the bank's investment in the event the contractor goes out of business or simply fails to complete the work.

Many communities have an extensive construction approval process requiring use and zoning variances. The use and other applicable variances will need to have been obtained before the loan process begins. A lending institution does not want to spend time and man hours on a loan for a building that may not be approved for construction. Frequently, variances have a specific time frame associated with them. It is imperative the borrower stays on top of the variance's expiration dates. The borrower may have to request variance extensions throughout the loan process.

If the future construction is going to be built on land which the borrower does not yet own, a contract to purchase the land will need to be solidified. As noted under the contract portion of the loan application, the bank will want to know the contract for sale is current and enforceable and its terms of purchase. A current survey of the property will also most likely be required, as well as a current title search.

8. THE BUSINESS PLAN

How does a business plan relate to a business loan? The business plan provides a lending institution a clear understanding of your business, the direction which you plan on taking your business and the process to obtain the results. A company with a well written business plan has a far greater chance of succeeding than a company without a plan.

The business plan is to a business what construction drawings are to a construction project.

Even though many aspects of the business plan are included in other sections of the loan application, it is important to submit to the lender the business plan in total. Many of the categories previously noted will be expanded on within the business plan.

A well written business plan will provide a lending institution with a clear and detailed understanding of what your company does, who the owners and management are, including experience and competencies, the direction in which you wish to take your business and the time frame it will take one to accomplish the task. Submitting a detailed business plan is an indication to the lending institution that a business owner is serious about his or her business endeavors. The opposite is also true; submitting a poorly written business plan or none at all will make the lender question whether one is serious about owning a business.

Business owners have an acute knowledge of their business and the industry in which they operate. This knowledge is more than likely on both a micro and macro level. Lending institutions may or may not have the same acute understanding of the business as the business owner does. The business plan is the entrepreneur's opportunity to provide this information.

A micro knowledge level is defined as how one is planning on operating his or her business locally and internally. A macro knowledge level is defined as knowing what is new in one's industry and how others operate businesses in other locales, including details on whether one is in a growth industry or a niche business. An example of a niche business is the buggy-whip business and an example of a growth business would be alternative energy.

Two industries that come to mind which have a very distinct micro and macro environment are the restaurant business and the child care or early childhood education industry. Both of these businesses rely on the local economy for their clients but, the industries are continually evolving.

> **There's no shortage of remarkable ideas, what's missing is the will to execute them.**
>
> *- Seth Godin*

The restaurant business on a micro level is continually creating a more unique experience for the patrons, in turn creating repeat business. On a macro—level it would be a thorough understanding of how technology is transforming the industry. One example of this technology is the hand held computers which are being used to place orders directly from a customer's table to the kitchen.

Early child care or early education is a localized business when it comes to the students each school serves. Each individual geographic location will initially meet the children at their need level and attract students from its local economy. On a macro level, how are changes in the industry as a whole affecting one's business? Use of technology is one example, as are the ever changing methods of educating children.

The important items that need to be in a business plan are the following;

1. **Executive Summary**
2. **Business description**
3. **Market Strategy**
4. **Ownership and management bios**
5. **Internal operational components**
6. **Competitive analysis**
7. **Financial analysis**

1] The Executive Summary:

The executive summary should only be one page, short and to the point. The reason is two-fold; the person reading the executive summary can quickly determine if the project fits the institution's lending criteria. All lending institutions have a lending limit and an expertise in specific business categories. The second reason is, the details that substantiate your comments in the executive summary will be in the contents of the business plan.

Specifically the executive summary should provide the name of the person and/or company submitting the business plan, the amount of the loan request, and a brief description of the business being financed, details on the transaction and, a brief synopsis of the management.

2] Business Description:

Within the Business Description category the business owner will provide details of the business and its product or service. The business owner should be very detailed and include such items as the history of the industry and business and what makes their business unique. A business owner should use his or her business savvy on what they would write for the history of a specific industry. For example: the history of the restaurant and tavern industry does not need to go back to the beginning. Establishments that provide food, beverage and entertainment have been around for centuries. One may want to describe details on the history of the industry for its specific area. What is unique about the locale that has drawn persons to this location or will in the future? For example, writing a business plan for a restaurant establishment in Atlantic City before the influx of casinos would be completely different than writing a business plan for a restaurant with its current influx of casinos. A new retail establishment that is offering goods in a brick and mortar store as well as an on-line presence would want to describe the on-line purchasing of goods and services from its inception and the continued impact it is having on the retail establishments.

3] Market Strategy:

A very important aspect of any business is how one obtains clients. Why is a potential customer going to enter your store or engage your company to spend money? In the case of a product, how are you going to bring your product to the market place? Customers are the driving force behind any and all products and services.

NAVIGATING THE LENDING MAZE

Without clients, the purchasers of one's product or service, there is no revenue and without revenue there is no company. If your product will require distribution channels how are you going to access these distribution channels? Will you need a sales force? If so, what are the criteria for the hiring of the sales people? Have you completed any type of test marketing to determine the interest in your product, and if so, what are the results? In the event the product or service is internet based have you completed a beta test? In the event your product or service is already accepted in the market place, such as children's clothing for example, a market strategy would be directed more towards why someone would buy clothes from you in lieu of someone else. What is unique about your product or service within in the marketplace? All of the above need to be answered under the heading Market Strategy.

4] **Ownership and Management Biographies:**

Even though the biographies of ownership and management are included in section 2 of the loan application as a standalone document, the business plan should have them included here as well. This section of the business plan will also provide details on the employees one will need for his or her business. The level of education and expertise required to fulfill employment at your company will determine how extensive one's employee descriptions are in this category.

For example: In the event one's company requires highly skilled persons such as design engineers, licensed nurses, experienced managers, how one will locate theses employees should be noted. If this is a buy-out of an existing company and the employees are in place, specifics on how one is going to retain these employees needs to be included. For companies requiring less skilled employees the borrower does not need to be as detailed.

A lender is relying on the competencies of the owner, management and employees for a company's success inclusive of a company's ability to repay the loan according to the terms of the loan. A borrower should utilize this section to provide the lender a comfort level that his or her company can and will be properly staffed.

5] Internal Operational Components

There are five distinct stages to all businesses irrespective of the type of business one owns and operates. The differences are; the complexities within each category, how each category is executed, the cost to manage them and the skill set necessary for those responsible for each category.

The five categories are:

1. Introduction
2. Proposal
3. Engagement
4. Fulfillment,
5. Payment.

The goal of each business is to effectively manage these categories for the purpose of providing a quality product or service to its clients and ultimately turn a profit.

The coordination of the five business components, the means by which a customer moves through the different phases and the proper execution of each category are the Internal Components of a business. Remember, one is not just writing a business plan for the lender; all of this is being written to provide a roadmap for one's company as well. Knowing how all of the internal components of a business are coordinated will provide the business owner with far greater percentages of success.

> " A business has to be involving, it has to be fun, and it has to exercise your creative instincts. "
>
> *- Richard Branson*

4] Fulfillment

As the saying goes, "This is where the rubber meets the road". Fulfillment is the phase where a business provides the product or service which the business was established to furnish. The parameters within this category are as diverse as the products or service which a company provides.

For a manufacturing business this may appear to be somewhat simple--a description of how raw material moves through the manufacturing facility. For other businesses it may not seem to be as obvious. For example, a surgery center would describe how a patient moves through the pre-operative stage through the surgery and into the post-operative stage of the procedure.

5] Competitive Analysis

Competition needs to be viewed as being a healthy aspect of owning a business. It is one of many benchmarks by which your business will be evaluated. An existing business looking to expand or grow the business will have a history on which to expand. If sales are trending up this makes the explanation very easy. If a business's sales are trending down a business owner is going want to establish a distinct plan on how to reverse the trend.

At the very least a thorough analysis of one's competition will address the following questions:

1. Why is someone going to knock on my door instead of my competitor's door?
2. Who is your competition and how will you be better than your competition?
3. What is your unique selling proposition?
4. Is your market place growing or will you need to siphon business from your competition?

A restaurant will have a different competitive analysis than a manufacturer or an ambulatory surgery center. The restaurant may look at a type of food not offered in the area. The construction of new offices or a new residential real estate development could very easily increase the demand for restaurants. Retail stores need to be concerned with more than just the competition in the local geographic neighborhood. With the proliferation of internet sales over the years, competition is bigger than the store around the corner. Products can now be purchased from the comfort of one's own home.

How one's business is going to address the competition is an important part of the business plan.

6] **Financial Analysis:**

There are many ways to analyze a business financially.

The most basic and fundamental rule in business is: one must take in more money than one spends. This simple financial analysis is located within the profit and loss statement. The profit and loss statement will quickly provide someone with knowledge on whether a company is profitable or not.

The profit and loss statement is only one of the numerous financial documents that should be located within the business plan. The financial documents should not be placed in the business plan as filler to satisfy requirements for a loan application. The documents should be placed in the business plan to provide a financial road map and tool by which to analyze a company's finances for the purpose of becoming and remaining profitable. This tool called a business plan is the document which a business owner should be referring to on a regular basis for the purpose of building a strong business, much like a builder refers to blueprints for the purpose of correctly building a structure.

The following documents should be included in the business plan:

1. Profit and Loss Statement for the previous three years
2. Balance Sheet for the previous three years
3. Two years business projections, sometimes called Pro-formas
4. Cash Flow analysis by month for a new business
5. Expense Analysis
6. Accounting of clients and how they relate to a company's revenue
7. Break Even analysis

9. FINANCIAL STATEMENTS

The previous three years of Profit and Loss Statements and Balance Sheets will provide a financial snap shot at twelve month intervals. They will need to be included with the loan application. The interim financial statements will provide the lending institution with a very recent snap shot of a business's financials. The interim financial statements will provide the lender with the most recent snapshot of a company's finances. The interim financials should not be any older than 60 days. The interim financial statements should include a Profit and Loss Statement and a Balance Sheet.

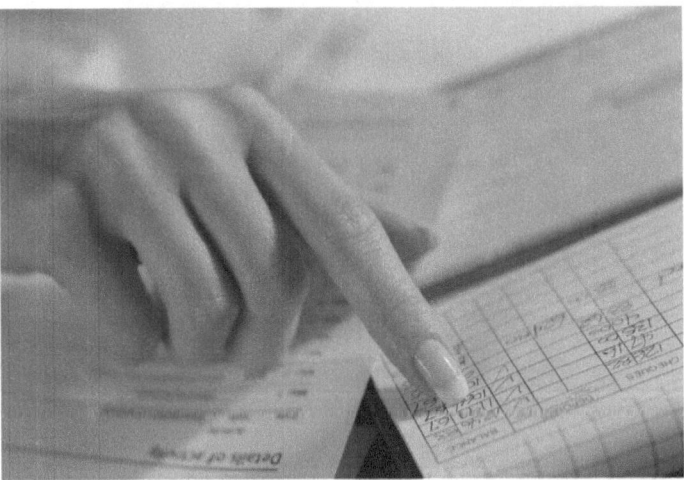

For new companies that are frequently called start-ups there will not be any interim financials. The loan will be based upon other financial information, specifically business projections which are covered in Chapter 13. When an existing business is being purchased, the seller will need to unconditionally cooperate with the buyer and the lender and provide interim financials.

10. SCHEDULE OF BUSINESS LIABILITIES

Having debt is a part of being in business. The ability to manage the debt is also a part of being in business. Too many business liabilities for a company can be financially troublesome. There are both long term and short term financial obligations. For example, long term business obligations could include a mortgage on one's business property. Short term business obligations would be debts that are structured to be paid off in fewer than twelve months. Loans such as credit lines and vendor credit are considered to be short term loans. Most if not all vendor credit is paid off within 30-90 days. A Schedule of business liabilities will provide the lender with insight on how much indebtedness a specific company has and how they manage the debt.

---

*"Your income is directly related to your philosophy, **NOT** the economy."*

Jim Rohn

---

11. AGING OF ACCOUNTS RECEIVABLE (AR) AND ACCOUNTS PAYABLE (AP)

Accounts Receivable is the money which is owed to a company and Accounts Payable is the money that is owed by that company to others. How long a company takes to pay its bills and how long it takes to get paid is known as "aging of accounts." Aging of both payables and receivables have a direct relationship on a company's cash flow.

Having accounts receivable that are too old will have an adverse effect on one's ability to pay one's obligations. A large volume of Accounts Receivable that are over 60 days approaching 90 days are considered old. Receivables that are fewer than 30 days are considered current. This is an indicator of how a company provides credit to its clients and how responsive its clients are in paying those bills. Many industries have trends in Accounts Receivable; some are traditionally paid in 10-45 days and others are paid in 6-9 months. An example of a 10-45 day accounts receivable is a lumber yard, and an example of one that has 6-9 months is a medical professional that relies on insurance company payments.

Aging of Accounts Payable is an indicator of the time frame in which a company pays its financial obligations. Financial obligations that are current indicate a company's cash flow and ability to manage credit, all of which are positives when applying for a loan.

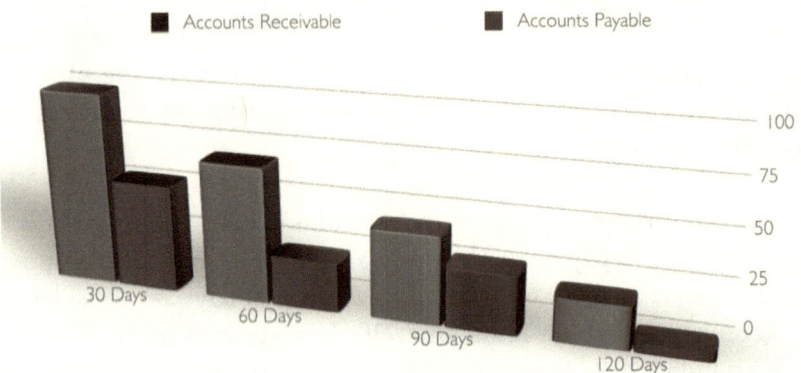

12. OUTSIDE CONSULTANTS

The use of an outside consultant can be an asset to one's company. The reason companies hire an outside consultant, sometimes referred to as an advisor, is for their expertise. When engaging an outside company or person their background and credentials should be submitted. This information will enhance the loan application.

How To Hire An Outside Consultant

What & When

Outside consultants are individuals and companies that have an expertise in a specific business genre or niche. A company hires an outside business consultant when a need arises that requires a depth of expertise that the staff and management lack, yet the need does not necessitate a new hire.

A few familiar examples include an attorney to assist a business completing a transaction and an accountant to complete the required quarterly reports or tax returns. Most firms that are considered small businesses do not have the finances to afford a full time in-house attorney or a full time accountant. These firms rely on the expertise of outside consultants to assist in operating a high quality company. A small business owner needs expertise in two major areas-- the expertise in the product or service in which the company is engaged and the knowledge of how to run a successful business. He or she cannot be an expert in all aspects of a business and should not feel that they should be. Throughout the years I have seen consultants hired to resolve temporary challenges, including CFO's, CEO's, human resource issues, to obtain financing and to complete lengthy government pre-qualification applications.

Who & How

The question always becomes whom to hire. There are actually two questions here. The first question is how to find an appropriate consultant and the second is analyzing their qualifications when hiring them. A pre-qualified referral is always the best way to locate a company or individual to fulfill the need. There are several places to obtain these referrals. One is a company's accountant and attorney. Both of these professionals usually have a diverse client base and know someone that will fill a company's requirements. Another good place is a Chamber of Commerce. Personally I prefer regional Chambers of Commerce, as their members seem to be more diverse. A third place is a business owner's own professional sphere of influence. A business owner should frequently be connecting with other small business owners to establish a well-rounded sphere of influence and business contacts. Consider also consulting presidents of your industry trade or professional associations, or trade magazine editors.

After candidates have been selected an interview process begins. Even before the interview process begins a scope of work should have been established. This allows both the hiring company and the company being interviewed a means to determine if there is a good fit for both. A quality company, even though they have good credentials, may not have the expertise to fulfill the needs required. Many companies act on price alone; this is not always in anyone's best interest. The key is value and any consultant should be bringing value to the hiring company. A company that may be more expensive may provide a higher level of competencies than a lower priced company. This can only be determined after an interview process has been completed.

In today's business environment the internet cannot be ignored. Locating businesses on the internet is both a blessing and a curse. The internet has the ability to expose companies to a much larger group of clients, which has served the business community well. The internet has also provided companies with the ability to connect to much needed goods and services that they would not have been exposed to. The down side is that the business community has lost the personal touch, which in many instances is the best manner to hire someone to assist a business. When using the internet to locate companies, unless they come highly recommended by someone you trust, a personal interview is always in the hiring company's best interest.

13. BUSINESS PROJECTIONS

Lending institutions will request financial projections covering the next two years for the borrowing business. With two years of business projections coupled with the past three years Profit and Loss Statement and Balance Sheet (noted in number 12), as well as interim financials, a lender will have five years of financial information from which to evaluate a borrowing company's loan request.

Projections of future earnings and related expenses are one of the most difficult aspects of a loan application to verify. When an existing company is applying for the loan, history of past expenses will be a gauge of future expenses. Any additional expenses that will be incurred after the loan has closed should be included. Some of the new expenses could include loan, mortgage or interest payments. Businesses should be sure to eliminate expenses that will no longer exist once a loan has been obtained. For example, one such expense could be a rental payment that would be replaced by a mortgage payment.

The projections should not only include additional expenses; projections should note any increases in revenue that will result from obtaining a loan. All industries have a means of information gathering and documentation, providing industries with many different types of industry specific details. This information is vital in determining a product or service's demand, market share and, the probability of being profitable. For example, the auto industry has a reasonable understanding of how many cars should be sold in any given geographic area; the hotel industry has documentation on how many rooms are available; the room occupancy percentages and rates; and, the medical industry has data pertaining to whether another surgery center is required in any given area. This information can be used to verify one's projections.

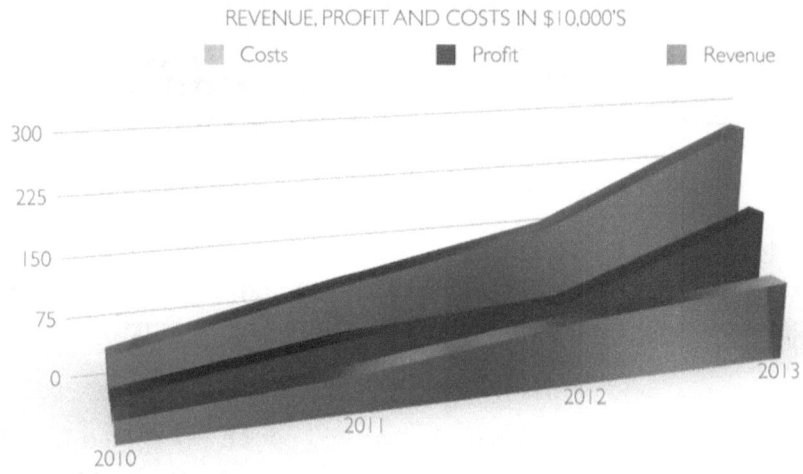

Industry information will provide averages; and, as with all averages, companies are above the average and below the average. A business owner will need to make an argument for why his or her business will be above the industry averages.

New businesses without a track record will be underwritten completely on financial projections. Frequently these loans are named Pro-Forma Loans. As one would anticipate these loans are the most difficult to underwrite and subsequently take more time than any other type of loan to process. The borrower should expect to, in most cases, pay a higher interest rate, as well.

14. BUSINESS TAX RETURNS

The lenders will require three years of business tax returns. The tax returns will include the borrowing company and, if this is a business acquisition, the tax returns of the company being acquired will need to be included.

In the event this is a new business there will not be any tax return and the projections noted under Chapter 13 will be relied on to underwrite the loan. When an existing business is purchasing another business the tax returns of the existing business will need to be submitted.

If existing business owners are purchasing another business unrelated to their existing company, the tax returns of the existing business will need to be submitted. This would then be included under Chapter 15 additional businesses.

> *To succeed in business, to reach the top, an individual must know all it is possible to know about that business.*
>
> *- J. Paul Getty*

Financial information in the tax returns is the most widely used in analyzing a company's financial where-with-all. The profit or loss on the returns is not the only number the lenders look at. The underwriters are reviewing the returns for items which can be added back in to justify providing a company with a loan.

NAVIGATING THE LENDING MAZE

What are items that can be added back in? They are expenses that will either be eliminated by the loan--such as rent (when business property is being purchased in which to house one's company), or expenses that are deducted from a company's income, which are not paid from a company's revenue, such as depreciation.

15. OTHER BUSINESSES

Other Businesses are defined as: businesses that any owner of the borrowing company has a 20% or more ownership interest in.

Lenders will require complete financials on what are defined as Other Businesses even if the businesses do not have an ownership interest in the borrowing company. The reason being, the lenders want to have a thorough understanding of the borrowing company owner's global or complete financial status. There are numerous reasons for this request. One reason is to determine whether the owners are successful business owners. Another reason is to determine if the other businesses are losing money and if so, will the money borrowed be siphoned off to support a business that is not profitable?

> Even if you are on the right track, You'll get run over if you just sit there.
>
> - *Will Rogers*

The opposite is true as well. If one of the owners and subsequently one of those signing the note has a business that has strong financials, this will have a positive effect on the loan analysis and increase the probability of a loan approval.

The financials that will be required are; 3 Years of Federal Income Tax Returns, 3 Years of Profit and Loss Statements, 3 Years of Balance Statements and interim financials that are not any older than 60 days.

16. CREDIT

Credit worthiness is an important aspect of borrowing money. A lender will request a credit report on all persons who will own 20% or more of the borrowing company. Lenders cannot accept credit reports that are submitted by others; they are required to use a credit report which they obtain themselves.

It is recommended that borrowers obtain a credit report for themselves before they apply for a loan. This way the borrowers do not have any unexpected derogatory issues on the credit report. Judgments and or tax liens have an adverse effect on one's loan application. It is advisable to pay them off before a loan is applied for.

All lenders have different credit score cut-offs. Many lenders will accept or continue with a loan application if the borrowers have a credit score of 650 or more. Other lenders will require a credit score of 700-750 before they move forward with a loan application. The higher the credit score the more credit worthy a borrower is; the opposite is also true.

Along with the credit score a personal background check will be completed. The lenders will be looking for any criminal records or other issues that have an adverse effect on your character. At times even the smallest of infractions have come up with background checks. This includes those infractions that have been expunged.

When the borrower is in a licensed profession such as an attorney, doctor, accountant, etc., the borrower's license will also be checked to see they are in good standing. A lender will be reticent to provide a loan to a licensed professional who has been sanctioned in some form.

17. LEASES

Copies of all leases will need to be submitted. This includes lease obligations the borrowing company has with others and lease obligations in which the borrowing company is the lessor. When the borrowing company is leasing the property from which it will operate its business, the loan cannot be longer than the term of the lease. If it is a five-year lease, the loan cannot be longer than five years. If the lease is five years with a five-year option, the loan can be upwards of ten years.

For a single tenant property in which one company rents the entire property, frequently the finances of the leasing company will need to be submitted with the loan application. It is imperative when writing a lease that the owner of the property has the right to request and receive financials upon request.

Property being leased by the borrower will need to be leased at a minimum for as long as the length of the loan. A lender wants to be confident the borrowing company will be in the building to operate their business for a minimum time frame to effectively repay the loan.

When a lease is submitted with a loan application, the entire lease needs to be submitted. The lease is evaluated to insure the lease is still cost effective years after the initial lease date.

18. SOURCE OF CAPITAL INFUSION

Source of Capital infusion is often referred to as the down payment. The simplest form of a Capital Infusion is cash or another form of liquid asset that can be easily converted to cash.

There are other means by which to obtain the capital Infusion that should be noted here.

If the borrower owns property that can be refinanced or leveraged, the funds obtained from this type of loan can be used as a capital infusion. If this is the approach used, it should be noted that the debt service of this loan will need to be figured into the overall debt service coverage ratios of the entire project.

An acceptable but more complex means to obtain the capital infusion is from monies previously expended on the project the borrower is seeking funds for. Not all monies spent on a project can be credited towards the capital infusion. In some situations the increase in the value of real estate can be used as the capital infusion. However, there are restrictions to using the increase of the value of real estate. One rule of thumb to follow is, the value of the real estate will be the purchase price when the loan is being applied for within 24 months of the land purchase. This is the case even if the property was purchased at a large discount compared to its appraised value. After twenty- four months the difference between the appraised value and the current indebtedness can be used as a portion of the capital infusion.

19. IDENTIFICATION

Within today's financial and lending environment a color photo ID will need to be furnished. The identification will not need to be submitted at the time of the application; it will need to be furnished before the loan can be closed. Acceptable identification examples are a current driver's license and current passport. Identification documents that have expired are not acceptable. This is a legal requirement and cannot be changed.

Provisions are made for those persons who are not United States citizens though are in the United States legally. In lieu of a current passport a green card is required to be submitted. Both the front and the back of the green card are submitted. The information is submitted for verification and when it is verified the loan closes without problems.

20. THE LIGHT AT THE END OF THE MAZE

A borrower's submittal preparation is an important aspect of the loan underwriting process. An organized, well collated and complete loan application makes the process smoother and goes a long way to minimize surprises during the underwriting process. The previous 19 chapters detail the items the lenders will be requesting from the borrower. Each bank and non-bank lender has its own nuances in the lending process.

The information once submitted is than analyzed and transposed into what I like to call "bank language". This process will accurately describe the borrower's needs, objectives and ability to fulfill the loan requirements in a manner that the loan underwriting committee will easily understand. A borrower's loan is approved or denied by persons whom the borrower will never meet. When a borrower engages the services of a qualified loan intermediary, the translation process runs even smoother, as the intermediary acts on behalf of the client to assist in positioning the loan for acceptance by a loan committee in conjunction with the bank's representative.

The information does not end with the borrower's submittals. There is often more information requested, and there will always be questions concerning the information submitted.

> **" I had to make my own living and my own opportunity! But I made it! Don't sit down and wait for the opportunities to come. Get up and make them! "**
>
> *- C.J. Walker*

The lending institutions will obtain certain documents themselves. These documents are in addition to the ones the borrower has previously submitted. The four most frequent documents are: a credit report, an appraisal, a business valuation and a feasibility study. Not all transactions will require all of them; all transactions will require some of them. The credit report will be ordered for every transaction. A borrower submitted credit report is not acceptable to the bank. There is not any harm in the borrower submitting a credit report obtained by one of the credit reporting services at the beginning of the transaction. This does provide the bank an initial understanding of one's credit worthiness. A borrower obtained credit report does provide the borrower with something to evaluate the bank's credit report with, in the event there is a vast difference.

A feasibility study is an analysis pertaining to whether or not there is sufficient valuable business to support your company. This is typically ordered when a borrower is opening a new business. An existing business has historical information to determine the viability of the market place. All industries have a means to evaluate potential business. This feasibility will be compared to the pro-formas submitted under Chapter 13. The projections noted with the feasibility study will prevail.

If a real estate purchase is involved, an appraisal is used for determining the value of land or of a building. The lender will order an appraisal from one of their approved appraisers. This is an independent determination of the current value of the real estate being financed. Property is financed at what is called Loan to Value or LTV. The difference between the

NAVIGATING THE LENDING MAZE

LTV and the price of the real estate is the required down payment. For example, if a building's purchase price is $100,000.00 and the LTV is 90%, the down payment required will be $10,000.00. Depending on the type of loan a borrower applies for and the type of property requiring the funding, LTV's can range from 50%-90%.

A business valuation is the determination of value of what a business is worth and is completed by a certified business valuator. This is a specialty and all banks have a list of those who are approved. Not only do the banks have an approved list, but industries have their specialists which are considered experts in their field and their values are held in high regard. Today's business environment has many companies with a great cash flow but requiring few assets to operate. Technology and the internet have created this scenario. These companies are the most difficult to value and the most difficult to obtain loans for. The reason they are difficult to value and difficult to obtain loans for is the concern that the cash flow can quickly disappear. Also, many of them lack hard assets the lender could attach in the event of a default on the loan. Loans for these types of companies are usually funded by non-bank lenders with a specialty in the specific industry the borrowing company is involved with. Banks have not yet determined how to effectively value these businesses and continue to adhere to the constraints of the bank regulators. Having some form of cross collateralization and/or a strong financial means does increase the likelihood of obtaining a loan.

One of the most important items to be aware of during the loan process and documentation submittal is full disclosure. If there is an item you believe could inhibit you from getting a loan do not take the risk of not disclosing this at the beginning of the loan process. The item could very well show up later and derail the loan or delay the process for long periods of time. A questionable item either on one's credit report or background check willingly shared with the lender or the loan intermediary at the beginning of the process frequently can be tempered, as opposed to having to not only explain the item but now having to explain why it was not disclosed.

When a borrower has a low personal net worth or is considered a weak borrower a co-signer can be used to make the lender more comfortable with the security the loan will be paid according to the terms of the loan agreement. This a great benefit to persons who are borrowing for the first time and/or the co-signor can bring additional business knowledge to the transaction. A co-signer is a person who is liable for the loan repayment if the loan goes into default.

As noted in Chapter 14 Business Tax Returns, the information in the tax returns is widely used in the loan process. No one likes to pay taxes and business owners work diligently with their accountants to avoid paying those taxes. This is a double edge sword. The same accounting practices that allow for the reduction of paying of taxes could be the same practices that will prevent you from obtaining the loan, as the company's finances appear weaker. Reducing your tax liability as well as having the necessary funds to borrow to expand your business can be a difficult balance to obtain. This is just one reason why keeping your accountant apprised of your business plans is important.

Navigating the loan maze comes down to a game of show and tell. The more you can show and tell to convince the lender you know your business, you have integrity and you are seriously committed to your own success, the greater the chances they will guide you out of the maze and champion your cause.

> **You have brains in your head. You have feet in your shoes. You can steer yourself, any direction you choose.**
>
> *- Dr. Seuss*

www.ingramcontent.com/pod-product-compliance
Lightning Source LLC
Chambersburg PA
CBHW021042180526
45163CB00005B/2236